ALL AROUND THE WORLD
CROATIA

by Kristine Spanier, MLIS

pogo

Ideas for Parents and Teachers

Pogo Books let children practice reading informational text while introducing them to nonfiction features such as headings, labels, sidebars, maps, and diagrams, as well as a table of contents, glossary, and index.

Carefully leveled text with a strong photo match offers early fluent readers the support they need to succeed.

Before Reading

- "Walk" through the book and point out the various nonfiction features. Ask the student what purpose each feature serves.
- Look at the glossary together. Read and discuss the words.

Read the Book

- Have the child read the book independently.
- Invite him or her to list questions that arise from reading.

After Reading

- Discuss the child's questions. Talk about how he or she might find answers to those questions.
- Prompt the child to think more. Ask: Much of Croatia borders the sea. Where is the closest sea or ocean to you?

Pogo Books are published by Jump!
5357 Penn Avenue South
Minneapolis, MN 55419
www.jumplibrary.com

Copyright © 2023 Jump! International copyright reserved in all countries. No part of this book may be reproduced in any form without written permission from the publisher.

Library of Congress Cataloging-in-Publication Data

Names: Spanier, Kristine, author.
Title: Croatia / by Kristine Spanier, MLIS.
Description: Minneapolis, MN: Jump!, Inc., [2023]
Series: All around the world | Includes index.
Audience: Ages 7-10
Identifiers: LCCN 2022019814 (print)
LCCN 2022019815 (ebook)
ISBN 9798885241915 (hardcover)
ISBN 9798885241922 (paperback)
ISBN 9798885241939 (ebook)
Subjects: LCSH: Croatia—Juvenile literature.
Classification: LCC DR1510 .S63 2022 (print)
LCC DR1510 (ebook)
DDC 949.72—dc23/eng/20220429
LC record available at https://lccn.loc.gov/2022019814
LC ebook record available at https://lccn.loc.gov/2022019815

Editor: Jenna Gleisner
Designer: Molly Ballanger

Photo Credits: CHUNYIP WONG/iStock, cover; Tibor Bognár/age fotostock/SuperStock, 1; Pixfiction/Shutterstock, 3; trabantos/iStock, 4; xbrchx/iStock, 5; Sergiy Vovk/Shutterstock, 6-7; Nino Marcutti/Alamy, 8-9; OlgaKok/Shutterstock, 10; John Lazenby/Alamy, 11; Lubos Houska/Shutterstock, 12-13tl; Bogdan P/Shutterstock, 12-13tr; Sergeleazar/Shutterstock, 12-13bl; Alexandr Junek Imaging/Shutterstock, 12-13br; trabantos/Shutterstock, 14-15; Kristina Kuptsevich/Shutterstock, 16 (fish); Fanfo/Shutterstock, 16 (yota); zeleno/iStock, 16 (mussels); YanLev/Shutterstock, 17; Fotoholik/Shutterstock, 18; Wandering views/Shutterstock, 18-19; Mo Wu/Shutterstock, 20-21; ZhakYaroslav/Shutterstock, 23.

Printed in the United States of America at Corporate Graphics in North Mankato, Minnesota.

TABLE OF CONTENTS

CHAPTER 1
By the Adriatic Sea 4

CHAPTER 2
Life in Croatia 10

CHAPTER 3
Food and Fun 16

QUICK FACTS & TOOLS
At a Glance 22
Glossary 23
Index 24
To Learn More 24

CHAPTER 1

BY THE ADRIATIC SEA

Would you like to swim near a waterfall? You can in Croatia! Skradinski Buk waterfall is part of the Krka River. Summers here are warm enough to swim outside. Welcome!

Skradinski Buk

Croatia is in southern Europe. The Adriatic Sea borders the west. The coast is 1,104 miles (1,777 kilometers) long. It is filled with **coral reefs** and underwater caves. More than 1,100 islands and **islets** dot the coast.

Dubrovnik is on the coast. Walls surround the city. They were built almost 800 years ago. They protected the city from enemies. Now, visitors can walk on top of the walls.

WHAT DO YOU THINK?

Do you think walls are a good way to protect a city? Why or why not?

The Dinaric Alps run along the coast. Dinara Mountain is here. It is the tallest mountain in Croatia. It is 6,007 feet (1,831 meters) tall.

DID YOU KNOW?

The land along the Adriatic Sea is called the Dalmatian Coast. Why? Croatia was once called Dalmatia. This is where Dalmatians came from!

CHAPTER 1

CHAPTER 2
LIFE IN CROATIA

Farmers grow **crops** in the northeast. Sugar beets, corn, and wheat are some. Farmers raise pigs, cattle, and **poultry**. Beekeeping is also important here. Bees **pollinate** crops. They make honey.

beekeeper

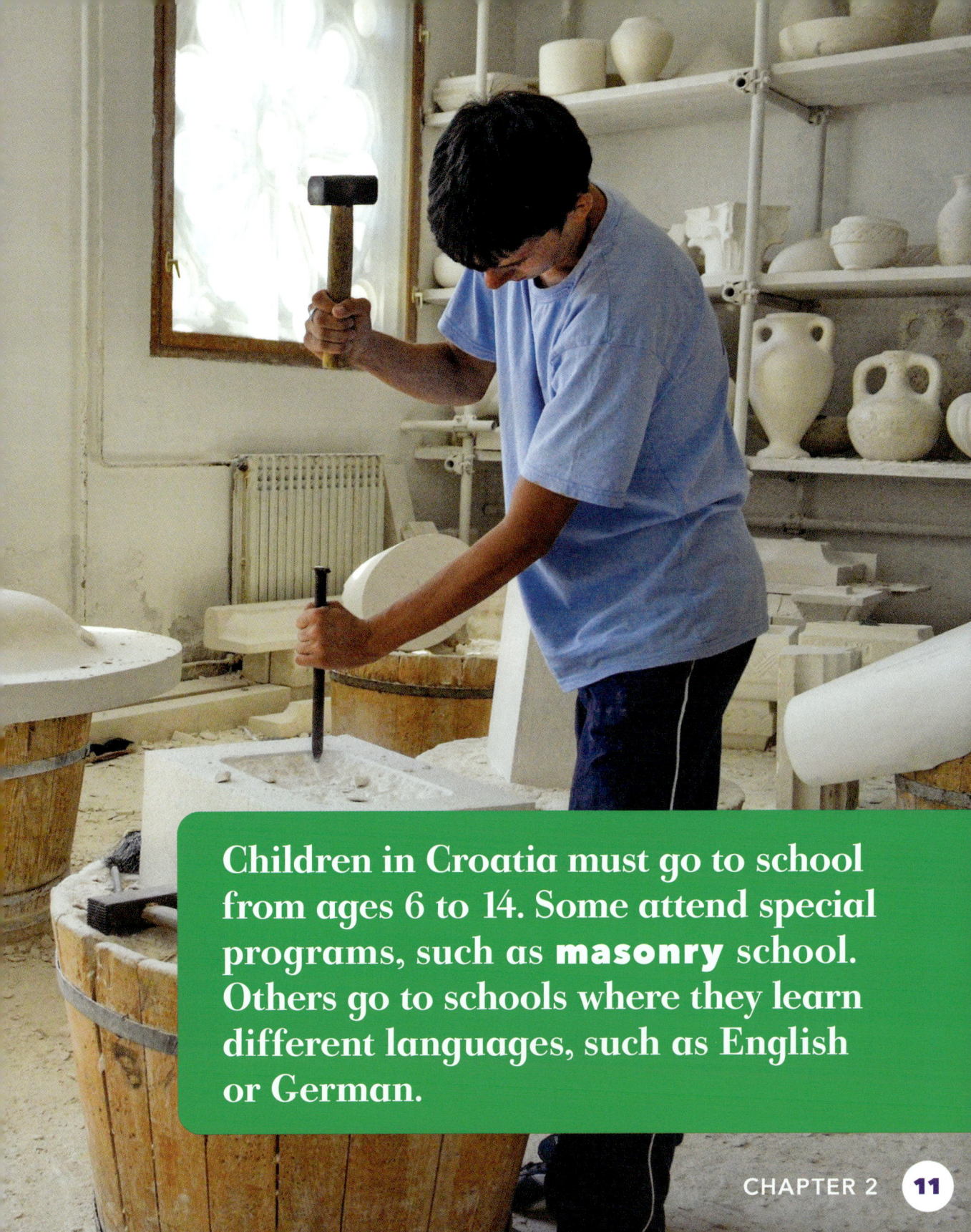

Children in Croatia must go to school from ages 6 to 14. Some attend special programs, such as **masonry** school. Others go to schools where they learn different languages, such as English or German.

long-eared owl

marten

chamois

river otter

More than 400 kinds of birds live in Croatia. The long-eared owl is one. Martens need to watch out for them! They find hiding spots in trees. The chamois lives in the mountains. River otters swim in the rivers and ponds.

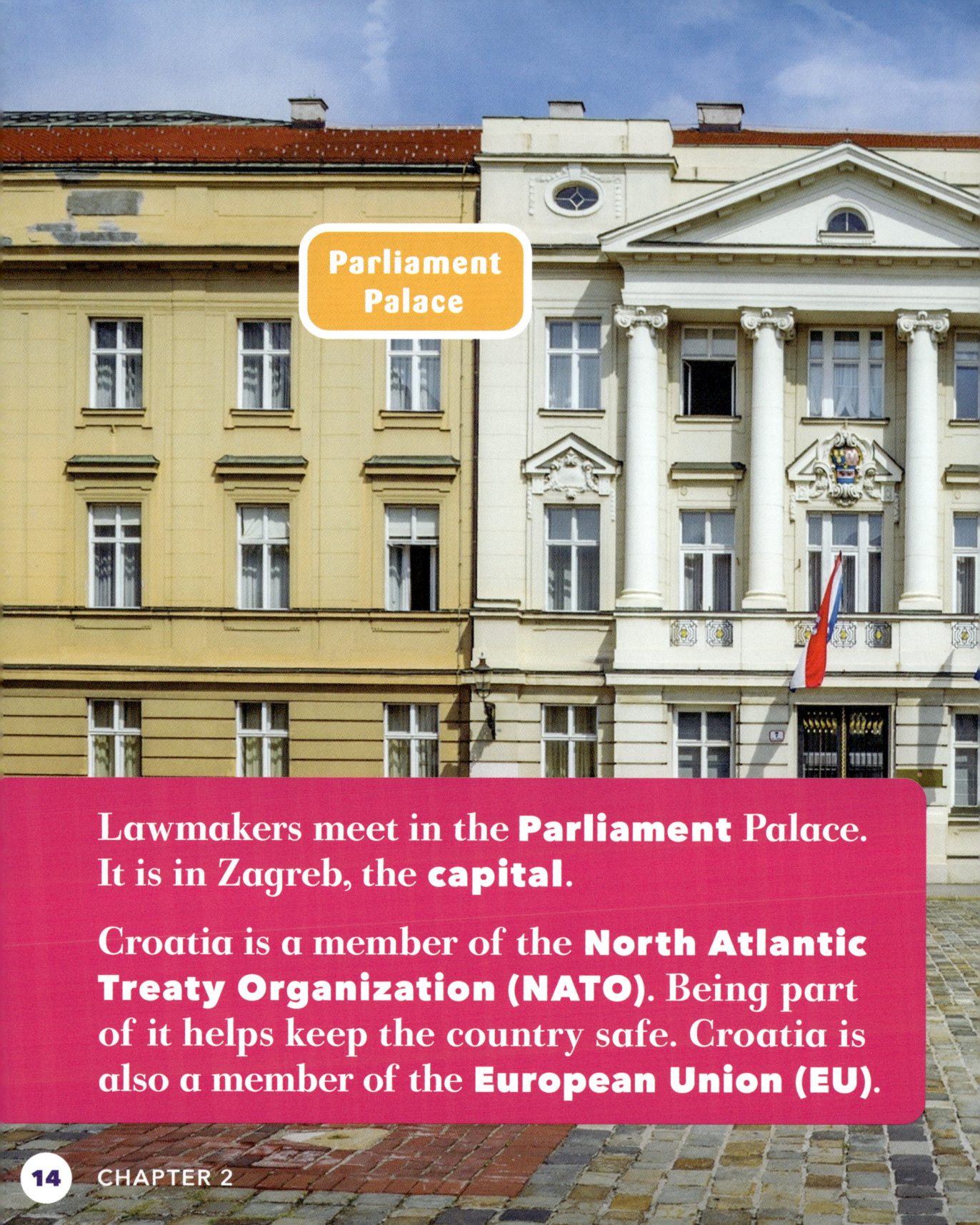

Parliament Palace

Lawmakers meet in the **Parliament** Palace. It is in Zagreb, the **capital**.

Croatia is a member of the **North Atlantic Treaty Organization (NATO)**. Being part of it helps keep the country safe. Croatia is also a member of the **European Union (EU)**.

TAKE A LOOK!

How does Croatia's government work? Take a look!

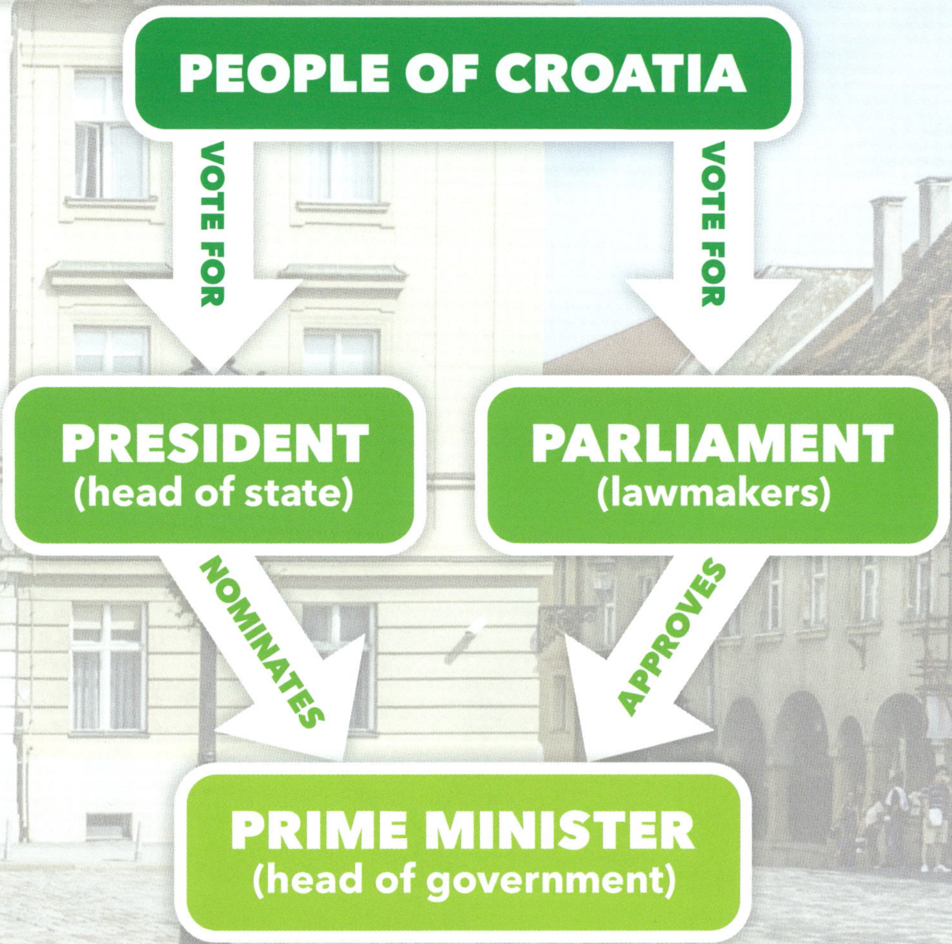

PEOPLE OF CROATIA

VOTE FOR ↓   VOTE FOR ↓

PRESIDENT (head of state)   **PARLIAMENT** (lawmakers)

NOMINATES ↘   ↙ APPROVES

PRIME MINISTER (head of government)

CHAPTER 3
FOOD AND FUN

The sea provides many tasty foods. Mussels and grilled fish are popular. The national dish is Istrian yota. This is sauerkraut stew with meat and beans.

Istrian yota

grilled fish

mussels

People enjoy water sports in the sea. Many swim, ski, and play water polo. Many people fish.

water polo

CHAPTER 3 17

In December, Christmas markets are filled with booths. People buy gifts and special foods. On Christmas Day, families enjoy large meals together. Fritule is a favorite dessert this time of year.

fritule

Christmas market

CHAPTER 3 19

The International **Folklore** Festival takes place in Zagreb. People from around the world come. They dress in **traditional** clothing. Musicians play the tamburica. It is Croatia's national instrument.

There is a lot to see and do in Croatia! Would you like to visit?

WHAT DO YOU THINK?

Dressing in traditional clothing is one way to remember a country's past. So is listening to traditional music. Why is it important to honor a country's history?

CHAPTER 3   21

QUICK FACTS & TOOLS

AT A GLANCE

CROATIA

Location: southern Europe

Size: 21,851 square miles (56,594 square kilometers)

Population: 4,188,853 (2022 estimate)

Capital: Zagreb

Type of Government: parliamentary republic

Languages: Croatian (official), Serbian, Hungarian, Czech, Slovak, Albanian

Exports: petroleum, medicines, cars, lumber

Currency: Croatian kuna

GLOSSARY

capital: A city where government leaders meet.

coral reefs: Long lines of coral that lie in warm, shallow waters.

crops: Plants grown for food.

European Union (EU): A group of European countries that have joined together to encourage economic and political cooperation.

folklore: The stories, customs, and beliefs of a group of people that are handed down from one generation to the next.

islets: Very small islands.

masonry: Building with stone, cement, or bricks.

North Atlantic Treaty Organization (NATO): An organization of countries that have agreed to give each other military help. This group includes the United States, Canada, and some countries in Europe.

parliament: A group of people elected to make laws.

pollinate: To carry pollen from flower to flower in order to make more seeds.

poultry: Farm birds raised for their eggs and meat.

traditional: Having to do with the customs, beliefs, or activities that are handed down from one generation to the next.

Croatia's currency

QUICK FACTS & TOOLS 23

INDEX

Adriatic Sea 5, 8, 16, 17
animals 13
beekeeping 10
children 11
Christmas 18
coral reefs 5
crops 10
Dinara Mountain 8
Dinaric Alps 8
Dubrovnik 7
European Union 14
farmers 10
foods 16, 18
government 15
International Folklore Festival 21
islands 5
islets 5
Krka River 4
languages 11
North Atlantic Treaty Organization 14
Parliament Palace 14
school 11
Skradinski Buk 4
sports 17
tamburica 21
Zagreb 14, 21

TO LEARN MORE

Finding more information is as easy as 1, 2, 3.

1. Go to www.factsurfer.com
2. Enter "Croatia" into the search box.
3. Choose your book to see a list of websites.